The Shoshone

Christin Ditchfield

Watts LIBRARY™

Franklin Watts
A Division of Scholastic Inc.
New York • Toronto • London • Auckland • Sydney
Mexico City • New Delhi • Hong Kong
Danbury, Connecticut

Note to readers: Definitions for words in **bold** can be found in the Glossary at the back of this book.

Photographs © 2005: AP/Wide World Photos: 46 (Laura Rauch), 20; Art Resource, NY/The Newark Museum, Newark, NJ: 11; Bridgeman Art Library International Ltd., London/New York: 3 left, 14 (New-York Historical Society, New York, USA), 32 (Royal Geographical Society, London, UK); Bruce Coleman Inc./F. Krahmer: 45; Denver Public Library, Western History Collection: 16 (X-32254), 36 (X-32256); Getty Images: 8, 18 (Otto Herschan), 35 (MPI); Gilcrease Museum, Tulsa, Oklahoma: 38 (*South Idaho Treaty*, by Charles Nahl); National Archives and Records Administration, Pacific Alaska Region, Seattle: 29; National Gallery of Art, Washington, DC: 13 (*Three Shoshonee Warriors*, by George Catlin, 1861, Paul Mellon Collection, Image © 2004 Board of Trustees); Nativestock.com/Marilynn "Angel" Wynn: 3 right, 6, 7, 9, 22, 23, 24, 25, 27, 33, 40, 42, 44, 48 bottom, 49, 50; North Wind Picture Archives: 30; The Image Works/Eastcott-Momatiuk: 48 top.

Cover illustration by Gary Overacre

Map by XNR Productions Inc.

Library of Congress Cataloging-in-Publication Data

Ditchfield, Christin.
  The Shoshone / by Christin Ditchfield.
      p. cm. — (Watts library)
  Includes bibliographical references and index.
  ISBN 0-531-12297-2
  1. Shoshoni Indians—History. 2. Shoshoni Indians—Social life and customs. I. Title. II. Series.
  E99.S4.D57 2005
  978.004'974574—dc22

                                                                 2005000630

Contents

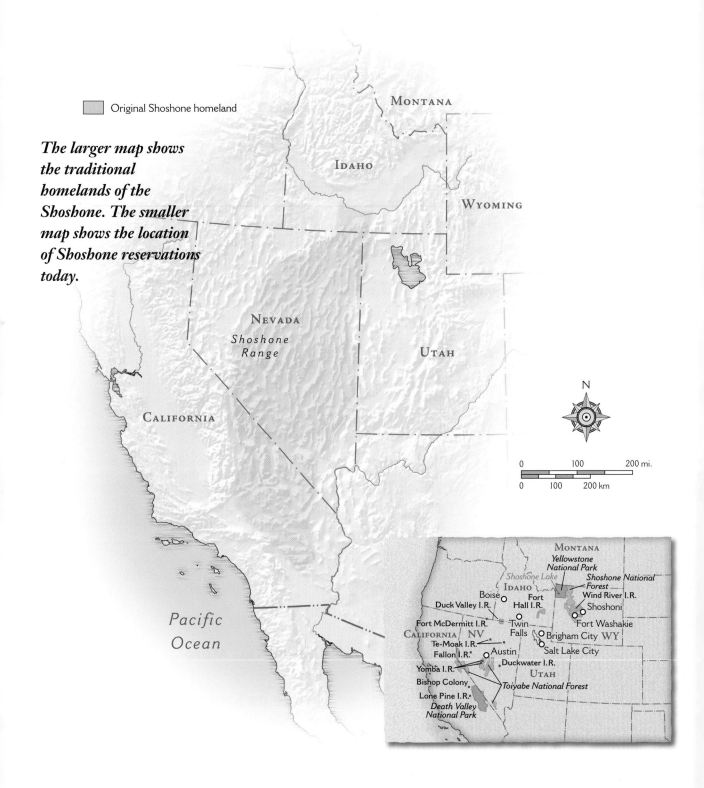

Original Shoshone homeland

The larger map shows the traditional homelands of the Shoshone. The smaller map shows the location of Shoshone reservations today.

MONTANA

IDAHO

WYOMING

NEVADA
Shoshone Range

UTAH

CALIFORNIA

Pacific Ocean

N

| 0 | 100 | 200 mi. |
| 0 | 100 | 200 km |

MONTANA

Yellowstone National Park

Shoshone Lake

IDAHO

Shoshone National Forest

Wind River I.R.

Duck Valley I.R.

Boise

Fort Hall I.R.

Shoshoni

Fort McDermitt I.R.

Twin Falls

Fort Washakie

CALIFORNIA NV

Te-Moak I.R.

Brigham City WY

Fallon I.R.

Austin

Salt Lake City

Duckwater I.R.

Yomba I.R.

UTAH

Bishop Colony

Toiyabe National Forest

Lone Pine I.R.

Death Valley National Park

Chapter One

People of the Great Basin

For more than one thousand years, the Shoshone people have lived in the western part of North America. The region in which they live is called the Great Basin, because it forms a giant bowl containing all the canyons and valleys between the Sierra Nevada and the Rocky Mountains. It covers approximately 200,000 square miles (518,000 square kilometers) and includes more than 160 groups of mountains.

For centuries, the Shoshone traveled seasonally from place to place throughout the Great Basin. They lived in valleys and on mountains, hills, and plains. Eventually, they divided into three large groups. The Western Shoshone lived in parts of Utah, Nevada, and California. The Northern Shoshone lived in northern Utah, Idaho, and Montana. The Eastern Shoshone lived along the Wind River in southern Wyoming.

A Nomadic Life

The Shoshone did not settle in one particular area. Instead, each group moved from place to place within its own territory. They were constantly searching for food. Very little rain fell on their side of the high mountains. They received as little as 5 to 7 inches (12.5 to 18 centimeters) of moisture per year. As a result, the valleys were often dry, sandy deserts. Nothing grew in large amounts or for very long. The land could not support large groups of people living in one place. There was simply not enough food or water.

To make finding food and water easier, the Shoshone broke up into smaller groups, or bands. A band was made up of

Shoshone

The word *Shoshone* (also spelled *Shoshoni*) may mean "valley dwellers." The Shoshone refer to themselves by using several similar-sounding words that simply mean "people."

several families, perhaps twenty or thirty people in all. Most of these bands did not have a chief or an organized system of leadership. Instead, the oldest and wisest members helped the band to make important decisions. Each band learned to make good use of the **resources** in its area. The Shoshone named

Many of the Shoshone lived in areas that were dry and desertlike.

7

The Shoshone lived in groups known as bands.

each band for the foods its people ate most often. For instance, some bands were known as "Salmon Eaters." Others were called "Rabbit Eaters" or "Big Sheep Eaters."

All Shoshone spoke the same language, but bands that lived in different areas developed their own beliefs and customs. They created their own ways of life, based on their surroundings. As a result, these individual bands sometimes had more in common with other Indian tribes living near their territory, than they did with members of their own tribe who lived much farther away.

Living off the Land

The Shoshone showed an amazing ability to adapt to the harsh conditions of the Great Basin. During the hot summer, they covered their skin with clay paste to protect them from the sun and insect bites. They learned which types of plants grew in certain areas during different seasons. Shoshone women knew which plants were **edible** or **medicinal**. They gathered pine nuts, ryegrass seed, roots, and berries, which they dried and baked into cakes. They cooked vegetables by placing them in little pits dug into the ground and covering the pits with rocks heated in a campfire. The Shoshone used some plants and herbs to treat illnesses. They used other plant

Roots and plants such as these were part of the Shoshone diet.

The Piñon Pine Tree

Every autumn, the Shoshone headed to areas where piñon trees could be found to gather pine nuts. The sweet, oily pine nuts could be shelled and roasted or eaten raw. The Shoshone often ground the nuts into powder and mixed it with animal fat and berries. The powder became a type of mush, or cereal, that could be eaten hot or cold. A family of four could gather as much as 1,200 pounds (448 kilograms) of pine nuts. This supply would last for months, feeding them throughout the long, hard winter.

fibers to weave baskets for storing and carrying food. Baskets coated with pine pitch (pine-tree sap) served as canteens to hold water.

Shoshone men hunted for elk, fish, rabbits, deer, birds, and bighorn sheep. Some went further out to the Great Plains to hunt buffalo. The Shoshone had to be skilled at using a variety of hunting tools and techniques. They hunted with bows and arrows, knives made of a hard black natural glass called obsidian, nets, and traps. Some had hunting dogs to help them corner animals and later drag the hides back to camp.

Hunters and Warriors

From time to time, the Northern and Eastern Shoshone hunted for buffalo. It was dangerous and difficult to do on foot. When they came upon a herd, the entire band would surround the buffalo in an effort to keep them from stampeding. They tried to corral some of the animals into a narrow ravine, trapping them in a canyon or up against the side

The arrival of horses in the 1700s changed the lives of the Shoshone.

of a mountain. Then the hunters would attack the buffalo one at a time, using lances or spears.

In the 1700s, the Shoshone acquired horses from other Indian tribes who had contact with the Spanish. This changed their way of life dramatically. They could now travel much farther and faster. It was much easier to circle the buffalo herds on horseback. Hunters could quickly move back and forth, swooping into and around the herd. The hunters threw spears or shot arrows as they rode by. It became possible to kill many buffalo at once, enough to provide food and clothing for the whole band. The hunters no longer had to worry about being caught in a stampede or charged by a wounded animal.

To develop more **efficient** hunting parties, the Northern and Eastern Shoshone formed larger bands that were more organized and had strong leadership. The most courageous and highly skilled men became tribal band leaders.

On several occasions, the Shoshone joined forces with the Bannock and Flathead tribes to coordinate even more massive buffalo hunts. But as they expanded their territory, the Shoshone came into conflict with other people of the Plains, such as the Arapaho, Blackfoot, Sioux, and Cheyenne. The Shoshone were not eager to fight. However, they could and would defend themselves.

Like those in other tribes, Shoshone warriors began wearing eagle-feather headdresses to reflect their accomplishments. Within the tribe, Shoshone warriors formed different groups. Young men belonged to the "Yellow Brows."

To prepare for battle, they painted their hair yellow, took a vow of bravery, and performed the energetic Big Horse Dance. Older, more experienced men belonged to the "Logs." They looked fierce with their faces painted black.

This sketch by George Catlin shows three Shoshone warriors around the mid-1800s.

The Comanche

One band of Shoshone called the Comanche, or "warriors of the plains," went to hunt buffalo one season and never returned home. Their **descendants** now reside in Oklahoma.

In the 1800s, some of the Shoshone chose to live in structures known as teepees.

Chapter Two

The Shoshone Family

As they traveled from place to place with the seasons, the Shoshone found many different ways to shelter themselves from the elements. In cold weather, some Shoshone lived in caves or shelters dug into hillsides. Some made cone-shaped lodges out of grasses, rushes, and willows. In the hot summer months, some built huts called *gahnees*, or lodges, out of sticks and branches. In the later 1800s, many Shoshone lived in tents called teepees. These were made of animal skins

A Shoshone woman wears a bead-and-shell necklace. The Shoshone would get some of their materials for jewelry and clothing through trade with other native peoples.

stretched over long, wooden poles called lodgepoles.

In the Great Basin, summer temperatures could climb higher than 100° Fahrenheit (38° Celsius). On hot days, the Shoshone wore very little clothing. Men wore loincloths made of deerskin or rabbit skin. Women wore aprons or skirts made of grass. The Shoshone went barefoot most of the time. However, if the ground was very rough, they would fashion sandals out of reeds or bark to protect the soles of their feet.

In the winter, temperatures often dropped below 0° Fahrenheit (-18° Celsius). Then the Shoshone wore thicker shirts or dresses and leggings made from animal skins. They bundled up in warm robes made of deer, elk, rabbit, or buffalo skins. The Shoshone traded furs to other tribes in exchange for seashells and beads made of bone or glass. They used the little ornaments to make earrings, necklaces, and bracelets and to create colorful floral patterns on their clothing. Both men and women pierced their ears.

Family Life

A Shoshone family usually consisted of one man, one woman, and their children. Several families living together made up a band. If there were more women than men in the band or if a man could afford it, a Shoshone man might take a second wife. Sometimes parents arranged their children's marriages, but usually young people were free to choose their spouses for themselves. The Shoshone had no formal wedding ceremony. A couple simply moved in together. Once they shared the same shelter, their bond was understood. For the first few years of their marriage, the couple often lived with their family, preferably the wife's. The man would prove that he could provide for his wife and eventually her family.

In the Shoshone family, each member played an important role. Shoshone men held the most respected positions. After all, they were responsible for protecting and providing for the tribe. Most bands did not have a chief, a chain of command, or any type of official authority. Decisions were discussed by the entire band, both men and women. However, it was always the men who took the lead on deciding issues that affected the well-being of the tribe. They rode into battle when necessary

Basket Weavers of the Great Basin

As expert weavers, the Shoshone combined different types of plant fibers to create baskets in different shapes and sizes. The baskets could be used as food storage containers, cooking pots, canteens, fish or bird traps, backpacks, and even hats. Other tribes were eager to trade with the Shoshone to acquire these useful objects.

Shoshone babies were carried on their mothers' backs in baby boards.

to safeguard their families and their land. The men hunted wild animals for food. The skins from the animals were used to make heavy winter clothing. The men crafted tools such as knives, bows, and arrowheads. Women, however, constructed the family homes.

Shoshone women were also respected members of the community. Without their special skills, the tribe could not survive. Shoshone women gathered more than one hundred different types of plants to use for food. They gathered another three hundred types of plants for medicines. The women made the family's clothing, jewelry, tools, and other household items. Shoshone women knew how to make pottery, but they were best known as expert basket weavers. For people who traveled constantly, lightweight, sturdy baskets were much more useful than heavy, fragile clay pots. Shoshone women raised the children. They carried their babies on their backs in frames made of willow branches covered with deerskin called baby boards. Each board included a shade made of woven willow.

Shoshone women could voice their opinion about matters that concerned the tribe, even though they did not have the final say. They earned greater respect as they became elder members of the tribe or as they demonstrated a particularly useful skill, such as healing or assisting in childbirth.

Shoshone children worked alongside their parents. Boys helped their fathers, and girls helped their mothers. Every member of the band did his or her part to hunt and gather food. It was the only way that the band could survive.

Celebrating Life

Although life was hard for the Shoshone, it was not all work. Families found time to laugh, play, and sing. In fact, singing was a favorite Shoshone activity. The Shoshone sang constantly throughout the day. They used drums, rasps, rattles, and flutes as instruments.

Tribe members expressed their creativity by crafting

Music and song were an important part of the Shoshone culture.

beautiful designs on their jewelry, clothing, and household items. At the hands of a Shoshone woman, even the most ordinary objects could be transformed into works of art. The patterns usually reflected the Shoshone's love of nature. Flowers were the most popular subject. On deer, elk, or buffalo hides, the Shoshone created pictographs, or paintings that explained their religious beliefs, described characters from legends, or detailed important events in the tribe's history.

The Shoshone also enjoyed playing many kinds of games.

Both male and female tribe members participated in these games, which included running relay races, conducting horse races, chasing hoops, throwing arrows at targets, and juggling mud balls. They even played a kind of football or American soccer called *shinny* with a ball made of animal skin that was stuffed with feathers. But the "hand game" was the most popular game. Several people secretly passed an object made of bone back and forth while singing. Another person tried to guess who was holding the bone. This game could go on for hours and could involve gambling for prized possessions, such as horses.

Harvest Time

At harvest or salmon-fishing time each year, Shoshone bands came together from all over the Great Basin. For some friends and family members, it was the first time they had seen each other in months. This was a time of celebration. Everyone

Sisters Save the Day

For centuries, Shoshone women were not allowed to play certain instruments (such as the drums) or participate in some of the ceremonial dances that were considered "for men only." But in the last thirty years the rules have changed. Fewer men know how to play the old songs and perform the traditional dances. Women have taken a leading role in preserving the Shoshone **culture**. They are keeping the memory of the old ways alive. On one occasion, a group of sisters performed the Giveaway and Chokecherry songs at a winter festival because no one else knew how. Without these women, the ceremonies could not have taken place.

Traditional crafts, such as beadwork, are still practiced today.

shared their family news. They introduced new babies that had been born in the last year. They remembered loved ones who had died. Children played games. Single young people looked for people to marry. This was the way most Shoshone found husbands or wives.

The annual festival often lasted for two or three weeks. Every evening, the people gathered around the fire. They sang, danced, and prayed. Sometimes they settled arguments or disputes between various bands. But mostly, they laughed and told stories late into the night. Because they had no written language, the young Shoshone learned their family histories by listening to older people tell stories about the past.

Annual festivals brought different bands together to celebrate and communicate with each other. Today, there are a number of annual festivals still held.

To the Shoshone, every part of nature, such as the mountains, has a spirit.

Chapter Three

Calling on the Creator

The Shoshone believed that the world was full of spirit beings. Every rock and tree, every mountain and lake, every animal had a spirit. All of the spirits were meant to live in harmony, coexisting peacefully together. According to Shoshone beliefs, there were also supernatural spirit beings that inhabited the sky and the earth. These spirits often intervened in people's lives. They guided and protected the Shoshone, giving them wisdom and pointing them to truth.

057807

The Legend Of Coyote

Coyote, or *Ishapah*, appears in the myths and legends of many western Indian tribes. This beloved character is a mischievous trickster, always getting into trouble with the other spirits represented by the animal kingdom. According to some myths, whether by accident or on purpose, Coyote was responsible for the creation of people. The Shoshone tell many tales of Coyote's adventures.

According to one story, Coyote hears a rumor that all the other animals are gathering at a council, where they intend to make him the most powerful leader ever. Coyote's head swells with pride. In his excitement he races all over the valley to find his brother Wolf, or *Ishá*. He can't wait to brag about the great honor that will soon be his. But Coyote can't find Wolf. He wears himself out searching for his brother. Exhausted, Coyote falls asleep in a thicket. When Coyote wakes up the next day, he discovers that he has missed the council. Wolf has been named leader in his place!

Every morning, the Shoshone prayed to the Creator. Some worshipped him as the Sun; others saw him as a spirit who took the form of Coyote. Many thought of the Creator as *Appáh*, "Our Father." They believed he would give them health and happiness if they honored him. Medicine men, or herbalists, were considered religious leaders and were often asked to help the Shoshone achieve mental and physical well-being. In addition, each person tried to get in tune with the great spirit.

The Shoshone constantly sought spiritual **guidance** through dreams. Throughout the year, they held ceremonies inside sweat lodges, which are dome-shaped huts made of sticks covered with animal skins, brush, and mud. Water was

poured over heated lava rocks to fill the lodges with steam. The moist heat was believed to cleanse and purify one's body, mind, and spirit. This made it possible to carry the prayers to Appáh. Today the Shoshone still use sweat lodges daily to ask Appáh for help in healing themselves, family members, and the tribe.

The tribe had a number of male and female healers who used roots and herbs, such as sage, cedar, and aspen bark, to

The Shoshone men sit outside a sweat lodge, which is a type of structure used for prayer and healing.

cure everyday aches and pains. The Shoshone believed that many illnesses were caused by bad spirits. To treat more serious cases, the healers called on the spirits to give them supernatural power through fasting and prayer. Then they attempted to remove the bad spirits from their patients by sucking them out or brushing or blowing them away.

Ceremonial and Social Dances

As part of their religious ceremonies, the Shoshone often danced together. The dances included the Round Dance, the Chokecherry Dance, the War Dance, the Warm Dance, and the Ghost Dance. Some of these dances took days to complete. Tribal members would often go without food or water as they focused their energy on prayers. Musicians accompanied the dancers with drums. Singers called out the words they believed the spirits had given to them, with the dancers repeating after them.

Each dance had its own meaning. Some were prayers for good crops, a successful hunt, safety, or healing. Other dances prepared the tribe for battle or celebrated a victory over an enemy. Still others were performed to give thanks or grieve the loss of life. Each dance had its own special steps and movements. For instance, for the Sun Dance, members of the tribe would leap or dance up to a center pole, then dance back in a large circle or shuffle in a huge circle around a tall pole. They prayed for their families and tribe for four days without food or water.

Peyote

In the 1800s, the Peyote Religion came to North America from Mexico. Peyote is a kind of cactus that, when chewed, alters a person's mental state creating visions. Many Shoshone embraced Peyote as a way to enhance their ability to communicate with the spirits. The cactus is still used in religious ceremonies by some members and bands today.

Children learned to do these dances at an early age by watching their parents and grandparents. Many of the ceremonial and social dances are still performed today, not only as a religious experience but as a celebration of Shoshone history and a symbol of the tribe's unity and spirituality.

A photograph shows the Sun Dance being performed at Fort Hall reservation in the 1920s.

The purchase of the Louisiana Territory expanded the United States. As a result, the United States took control of some of the lands that the Shoshone called home.

Chapter Four

The End of the Old Way

For centuries, the Shoshone lived peacefully in the Great Basin. Aside from occasional contact with trappers and fur traders, they had little to do with non-Indian peoples. Then in 1803, President Thomas Jefferson completed the Louisiana Purchase. For $15 million, Jefferson bought 827,987 square miles (2,144,485 sq km) of land in North America from France. This vast new U.S. territory extended north from the

The Lewis and Clark expedition benefited greatly from the help of the Shoshone and Sacagawea.

Gulf of Mexico all the way to Canada, and west from the Mississippi River to the Rocky Mountains. The land would later be divided into thirteen separate states.

In 1804, Jefferson sent a group of explorers, led by Meriwether Lewis and William Clark, to scout out the land beyond

Thomas Jefferson

Thomas Jefferson helped write the Declaration of Independence. He served as governor of Virginia, U.S. ambassador to France, and the nation's first secretary of state. In 1800, he was elected to be the third president of the United States.

Sacagawea

Sacagawea is one of the most famous American Indian women in history. In 1805, Sacagawea served with her husband as an **interpreter**. With her infant son Jean-Baptiste, or "Pomp," on her back, she traveled with the explorers Lewis and Clark through the wilderness across North America. This Shoshone woman showed more courage and strength than the forty-three men who traveled with her. More than once, she risked her life to save them. They later admitted that they could not have made it without her. In his journals, Lieutenant Clark wrote, "Intelligent, cheerful, tireless, faithful, she inspired us all."

In 2000, Sacagawea was **immortalized** on the U.S. dollar coin. The model for the coin was Shoshone-Bannock tribal member Randy'L He-dow (Meadowlark) Teton of the Northern Shoshone.

the Mississippi River. He wanted them to determine what opportunities might exist for the future growth and development of the country and to see if they could find a water route to the Pacific Ocean. Along the Missouri River, Lewis and Clark were joined by a young Lemhi-Shoshone woman named Sacagawea. They hired her and her husband, a French trapper, to serve as their interpreters. Sacagawea assisted the group in acquiring horses and securing safe passage through

Indian territory. She showed them how to identify edible and medicinal plants and where to cross the Rocky Mountains. With Sacagawea's help, the explorers not only survived their 8,000-mile (12,870-km) journey, but they discovered many of the wonders and difficulties of the West.

A Crowded Country

Soon the Shoshone encountered more than an occasional trapper or trader. Thousands of white people began moving into the Great Basin. Some passed through the area on their way to Oregon and the Pacific Coast on a route known as the Oregon Trail. Others were tired of living in the crowded cities in the East. They wanted to find a place in the open country where they could spread out and settle down—where they could build a new life for themselves and their families. The Mormons were a group of people who traveled west searching for a place to practice their religion. They established a large settlement in Utah, building their homes, ranches, farms, and towns right in the middle of Shoshone territory. The Mormons intended to live at peace with the Shoshone, and at first they did. But over time misunderstandings led to conflict and eventually to war.

When gold was discovered in California in 1849, a new wave of adventurers traveled west to seek fame and fortune. Silver was found in Nevada in 1859, and more gold in Idaho in 1860. Mining towns began springing up everywhere. These

towns took over lands on which the Shoshone and other tribes once thrived.

The land could not support all these people. The presence of many more hunters meant there was less game for everyone. Buffalo became scarce. The settlers cut down the piñon trees to build their homes, barns, and fences. Their wagon wheels crushed the plant life. They took large areas of land on which their livestock would graze. They also introduced new plants to the region.

The Mormons were one of the many groups that would eventually come into conflict with the Shoshone.

Washakie strived to make peace with the Shoshone's new neighbors, the settlers.

As the Shoshone traveled from place to place, they could no longer find the plants and animals they needed for food. The natural environment of the Great Basin was being destroyed, and so was the Shoshone way of life.

A Losing Battle

Some of the Shoshone fought to protect their lands and livelihood. Led by the prominent leader Pocatello, the Northern Shoshone launched a series of attacks on wagon trains, Pony Express riders, and railroad and telegraph construction workers. This led to a series of even greater conflicts between the settlers and the Shoshone. The settlers appealed to the United States government for protection. In one instance, the U.S. Army responded to Shoshone attacks by destroying a Shoshone village near Salt Lake City, Utah, in 1863. More than 250 Shoshone were killed in what became known as the Bear River Massacre.

Another Shoshone leader, Chief Washakie, saw that it was useless to try to drive the white settlers out of the region. There were just too many of them. The Shoshone were totally outnumbered. They did not have enough guns, horses, or warriors to mount an effective attack. The many different family bands were scattered and disorganized. Over the years, the Shoshone had fought when they had to, but they lacked any significant battle experience. This was a fight they could not win. Therefore, Washakie urged his people to make peace with their new neighbors.

Broken Promises

For the Shoshone, peace came at a great cost. They were forced to sign treaties agreeing to sell most of their land to the U.S. government. In 1863, the Northern and Eastern Shoshone signed the First Treaty of Fort Bridger. The Western Shoshone signed the Treaty of Ruby Valley. In signing these treaties, the Shoshone agreed to move onto **reservations**, which were specific areas of land set aside for them. In exchange, they were supposed to receive rations of food, medicine, and supplies they so desperately needed from the government.

However, the federal government did not always keep its promises to pay for the land it took. And it kept coming back for more. The size of the reservations were constantly being reduced, sometimes by millions of acres. This was the case with the Second Treaty of Fort Bridger in 1868. The Shoshone were forced to share what little land they had left with several other Indian tribes, including some of their fiercest enemies.

In the 1860s, the Shoshone were forced to sign treaties with the U.S. government. This painting depicts the signing of a treaty in 1866.

Eventually, white settlers took over nearly all of the Shoshone's land. The Shoshone could no longer live in the old way. The government suggested, and in some circumstances insisted, that the Shoshone become farmers. But the government failed to provide the Shoshone with the necessary tools and instructions to make this transition. The government also

Chief Washakie

Washakie was the most famous Shoshone leader. He led his people into battle against the Sioux, Blackfoot, and Crow Indians. At the same time, he developed friendly relationships with white settlers, trappers, and fur traders. He gained great influence with the U.S. government, and was able to negotiate favorable deals for the tribe. A man of his word, he kept his promises even when the government did not. Washakie established the Wind River Reservation in Wyoming. When he died in 1900, he was buried with full military honors at a U.S. Army fort that had been named for him.

did not take into account the fact that many of the reservations were located on land unsuitable for farming.

Over the years, the Shoshone had been weakened by conflicts with the U.S. Army and other warring tribes. They battled starvation and disease. Outbreaks of smallpox, measles, and tuberculosis had nearly wiped out the tribe. Yet throughout history the Shoshone had demonstrated a remarkable ability to adapt and survive even the harshest conditions. Today, the Shoshone population remains large, numbering in the thousands.

Despite facing many obstacles, the Shoshone population continues to thrive, numbering more than eleven thousand members.

Chapter Five

The Shoshone Today

Today, there are more than 11,000 Shoshone living in the United States. Many of them still live on one of eighteen reservations, colonies, or **rancherias** in Idaho, Wyoming, Nevada, Utah, and California. They share some of these lands with the Bannock, the Arapaho, the Goshute, and the Paiute. Other Shoshone have moved to cities and **suburbs** across the United States. In many ways, whether on a reservation or in a city, the Shoshone live just like any

41

Like children everywhere, many young Shoshone attend schools such as the Shoshone Bannock High School.

other Americans. They wear the same clothes and drive the same cars. They live in houses and apartment buildings. They work as doctors, lawyers, and engineers. Their children attend public schools.

The Shoshone still face some serious challenges as a result of the hardships their ancestors endured. Decades of broken treaties and empty promises have contributed to the tribe's economic troubles. The high rate of unemployment and poverty is a major concern, particularly for those living on reservations. It has not been easy for the Shoshone to preserve their heritage and at the same time adapt to the lifestyle of modern Western society. Those who have little contact with the outside world also have limited opportunities for their future. On the other hand, the Shoshone who are immersed in contemporary culture risk forgetting who they are and where they have come from.

Taking Care of Business

Since 1934, the United States has recognized the right of American Indians to govern themselves. In 1938, the Shoshone began organizing their bands or clans by creating tribal councils. Each council consists of a chairperson and six members elected by the band or clan they represent. These councils address community issues such as education, economy, employment, health care, and the prevention or punishment of crime. Separate business councils manage the tribe's resources, such as oil, gas, and uranium that are mined on Shoshone lands.

The Northern Shoshone have been very successful in their businesses, including shops, restaurants, and casinos. They have taken on a number of government projects and have made good use of the federal programs available to them. Of all the reservation lands allotted to the Shoshone, theirs is the most ideally suited for farming. Tribe members grow and sell potatoes, grain, and alfalfa. They even lease some of their land to other farmers.

The Eastern (Wind River) Shoshone live in or around the Rocky Mountains. The land is too rough and rugged for farming. However, members of the tribe are able to support themselves by raising cattle and breeding horses. They lease some of their lands to other ranchers for grazing. Many tribal members

This is one of the many farms that can be found on Shoshone lands.

Yellowstone National Park

In 1872, Yellowstone was declared the world's first national park. Once the site of an enormous volcano, the park features petrified forests and waterfalls as well as thousands of hot springs and hundreds of geysers. The land is surrounded by mountains filled with natural wonders and wildlife. The park covers more than 2 million acres (810,000 ha) in parts of Wyoming, Montana, and Idaho. A popular tourist site, Yellowstone is home to several Indian reservations, including that of the Eastern Shoshone.

work for the U.S. government in jobs that provide social services. Tourism also brings income to the tribe. Both the Yellowstone and Grand Teton National Parks are located in the area. Millions of people travel to the parks each year to enjoy the scenic beauty and catch a glimpse of the abundant wildlife. The region serves as home to deer, elk, moose, bear, and more than 280 species of birds, including the American bald eagle. The Eastern Shoshone operate a number of tourist-related businesses and serve as guides for those who want to go camping, hiking, hunting, or fishing in the area.

Carrie and Mary Dann are two of the many Shoshone battling the U.S. government for the return of tribal lands.

The Western Shoshone raise cattle. When their ancestors signed the Treaty of Ruby Valley in 1863, they agreed to keep the peace and "eventually" relocate to the reservations. However, the Western Shoshone were in no hurry to settle down. They just kept moving from place to place. They never did officially surrender ownership of their lands. They merely allowed the government to use them. Since the 1990s, the Western Shoshone have been involved in a lengthy battle to reclaim more than 22 million acres (891,000 ha) of land that was illegally seized by the U.S. government. Today the tribe is divided between those who think it is more practical and beneficial to accept money in payment and those who insist that the land itself should be given back to them.

Keeping Tradition Alive

Although in many ways they have become a part of contemporary American society, the Shoshone have worked hard to preserve their own unique history and culture. They are determined to pass on the Shoshone traditions to the next generation. Some have recorded elderly Shoshone telling the old stories and family histories. Others have created a written form of the Shoshone language so that it can be taught to young people. Some textbooks and dictionaries are now available in Shoshone. Furthermore, the Shoshone language is offered as a part of Idaho State University's curriculum.

Many Shoshone still hold their traditional religious beliefs.

Putting It on Paper

It is believed that Cameahwait, Sacagawea's brother, dictated the very first history of the Shoshone, which was written down in the 1800s.

Others are active members of the Native American Church, which combines elements of the Christian faith with American Indian traditions.

Museums and cultural centers display historical **artifacts**. They house samples of the tribe's traditional fine arts, basketry, pottery, tools, instruments, jewelry, clothing, and other items from the past. Larger reservations host rodeos and powwows to celebrate the Shoshone way of life. Tribal newspapers, magazines, and Web sites help members stay connected to each other and keep informed about issues that concern them.

By telling stories and teaching traditions, Shoshone elders pass along the history and culture of their people to the younger generation.

Tribal newspapers help the Shoshone share and convey information about events, news, and issues.

Sho-Ban News

NON-PROF
U.S. POST
POCATEL
PERMIT

75

www.shoban.

Owned by the Shoshone-Bannock Tribes

VOLUME 28, NUMBER 2   **COVERING IDAHO & INDIAN COUNTRY**   **FORT HALL,**
THURSDAY, JANUARY 8, 2004

INSIDE

▶ LOCAL

REBATE CARD

Enterprise rebate
System changes
                    Page 2

▶ LOCAL

Idaho water report
now storm brings in
.47 inches
                    Page 3

▶ SPORTS

Tornado believed to have flipped trai

By T'cha-Mi'iko
Sho-Ban News

A trailer house owned by R. L. Miller near Ferry Butte Road was destroyed late Monday night, Dec. 29th, during the big winter storm that tore through the area.

R. L. Miller, age 39, and his wife Karen Gould, age 37, made it out of the trailer after it had flipped over twice and landed upside down crushing the entire front end. Gould sustained a broken collarbone, cut, bruises and abrasions, Miller received cuts and bruises, but both were able to walk to neighbors to get help.

Meanwhile their neighbor, Danny Moss was with his family looking out at the storm, while his mother took the small children into the basement for safety.

"We could see nothing except for the flashes of

wind and watched the windows rattle and shake."

Moss said that all of a sudden they heard someone pounding on the door when they opened it they found Miller and Gould shivering and all battered looking.

had mentioned seeing a car spin off the road while they waded through the snow to Moss's house. When they were able to go out they found a woman in a car, stuck in a snowdrift across the road. She had barely

nado that hit here," said Miller. "It tossed a trampoline frame two hundred yards across the road into that field," he said as he pointed to a twisted frame lying in the snow-covered field.

Trailer rolled twice before being crushed on it's side on Ferry Butte Road during a lightning storm, which is believed to been in a path of a tornado touch down. (T'cha-Mi'iko photo)

over camper
was damaged.
The vehicle
opposite side
from the dest

Out in th
the road lay
smaller trail
through the
parts of it hu
roadside fenc

Moss said
neighbor bro
large tractor
move the wr
off the road
open a stret
Butte Road
gency vehicle
to take ou
injured Gould
Bingham Med

"It was h
around their t
thing was s
they will nee
place to stor
can salvage,"

Tribal
Access is tak

Celebrating the Past, the Present, and the Future

Every year in August, hundreds of people gather at the Northern Shoshone's Shoshone-Bannock Indian Festival. They sing and perform the old dances as well as the contemporary pow-wow dancing. They share traditional arts and crafts and play

A Shoshone woman performs a traditional dance at a powwow.

As part of the Fort Hall Indian celebration, participants compete in relay races.

hand games that the Shoshone have played for hundreds of years. There are rodeo events and Indian relay races. The popular festival also features parades, queen contests, and a softball tournament. It's a wonderful way to celebrate what it means to be Shoshone.

Timeline

1500s	From time to time, the Shoshone encounter European explorers and Spanish settlers. Their contact is limited.
1700s	At about this time, the Northern and Eastern Shoshone acquire horses and become buffalo hunters.
1782	The Eastern Shoshone barely survive an outbreak of smallpox and conflicts with the Blackfoot.
1804	With the approval of U.S. President Thomas Jefferson, Captain Meriwether Lewis and Lieutenant William Clark set out to explore the American West.
1805	The Lewis and Clark expedition enters Shoshone territory. A Lemhi-Shoshone woman named Sacagawea and her French husband become their interpreters.
1863	More than 250 Northern Shoshone are killed in the Bear River Massacre near Salt Lake City, Utah. The Northern and Eastern Shoshone sign the First Treaty of Fort Bridger with the U.S. government. The Western Shoshone sign the Treaty of Ruby Valley.
1868	The Shoshone are forced to sign the Second Treaty of Fort Bridger, which reduces the size of their reservations by millions of acres.
1900	Chief Washakie dies. The existence of the Eastern Shoshone is once again threatened by starvation and disease.
1934	The Indian Reorganization Act is passed in an attempt to secure new rights for American Indians living on reservations and to return self-government to them on a tribal basis.

1938	Across the country, bands of Shoshone formally organize, create tribal governments, and elect officials to decide matters that affect their welfare.
1972	The American Indian Movement (AIM) launches the Trail of Broken Treaties, a public demonstration against the unfair practices and policies of the federal government.
1993	The Shoshone and the U.S. government struggle to resolve conflicts over land rights and the protection of sacred sites.
2004	The House of Representatives passes the Western Shoshone Claims Distribution Act, paving the way for the federal government to pay the tribe $145 million for lands illegally confiscated in 1872.

Glossary

artifact—an object such as a tool or article of clothing used by human beings in the past

culture—the way of life, ideas, customs, and traditions of a particular group of people

descendants—relatives of people who lived long ago

edible—something that can be safely eaten

efficient—moving with energy and useful activity; not wasting time, effort, or expense

guidance—direction or advice

immortalized—made forever famous

interpreter—a person who speaks more than one language and helps others communicate by translating for them

medicinal—able to be used as medicine

rancheria—a farming community dedicated to raising horses, cattle, and sheep

reservation—an area of land set aside by the U.S. government as a place for American Indians to live

resources—supplies of things that people use to help them survive

suburb—a community of homes near or around a large city

To Find
Out More

Books

Bial, Raymond. *Shoshone*. Tarrytown, NY: Marshall Cavendish Inc., 2001.

DeKeyser, Stacy. *Sacagawea*. Danbury, CT: Franklin Watts, 2004.

Gray-Kanatiiosh, Barbara A. *Shoshone*. Edina, MN: ABDO Publishing Company, 2004.

Keller, Kristin Thoennes. *Shoshone: Pine Nut Harvesters of the Great Basin*. Mankato, MN: Capstone Press, 2003.

Marcovitz, Hal. *Sacagawea: Guide for the Lewis & Clark Expedition.* Broomall, PA: Chelsea House Publishers, 2000.

Mattern, Joanne. *The Shoshone People.* Mankato, MN: Capstone Press, 2001.

Moss, Nathaniel B. *The Shoshone Indians.* Broomall, PA: Chelsea House Publishers, 1997.

Ryan, Marla Felkins. *Shoshone.* San Diego: Blackbirch Press, 2003.

Santella, Andrew. *Lewis and Clark.* Danbury, CT: Franklin Watts, 2001.

Organizations and Online Sites

Eastern Shoshone Tribe
http://www.easternshoshone.net
This site includes information about the history and culture of the Eastern Shoshone as well as facts about the Wind River Reservation in Wyoming.

Lewis and Clark: The Journey of the Corps of Discovery
http://www.pbs.org/lewisandclark
On this site you can browse a list of the nearly fifty American Indian peoples encountered by Lewis and Clark during their

8,000-mile (12,872-km) journey. This site includes learning activities to help students relive the adventure of this historic expedition.

NativeWeb: Resources for Indigenous Cultures
Around the World
http://www.nativeweb.org
This site lists more than 4,000 historical and contemporary resources related to 250 separate nations.

Shoshone-Bannock Tribes
http://www.shoshonebannocktribes.com
This site tells about the history of the Shoshone and Bannock Indians, describes the annual Shoshone-Bannock Festival, and includes current news.

Shoshoni Dictionary
http://www.shoshonidictionary.com
This site contains an English–Shoshoni dictionary, as well as links to other Shoshoni language, history, and culture sites.

Utah History To Go
http://historytogo.utah.gov/shoshone.html
This site includes a good summary of the history of the Shoshone.

A Note on Sources

For thousands of years, the history of the first Americans went unrecorded. With no written language, tribes depended on oral tradition (storytelling) to pass on their heritage from generation to generation. By the 1900s, years of war and starvation and disease had decimated the native population. More than half of those who identified themselves as American Indians had left the reservations and were quickly absorbed into the general population.

Like many other tribes, the Shoshone recognized that their culture was in danger of disappearing. They developed special programs to educate tribe members about their history and heritage. They opened cultural centers and museums to preserve precious artifacts. They created newspapers, journals, and Web sites to give members of the tribe a sense of their identity and help them connect with one another.

The Shoshone have worked hard to preserve their history

for their own children and grandchildren. In the process, they have educated the rest of the world about what it means to be Shoshone. A young leader in the Shoshone-Bannock community, Randy'L He-dow (Meadowlark) Teton served as the model for Sacagawea on the golden U.S. dollar. Teton is widely recognized as an esteemed tribal member and spokesperson on Shoshone history and culture, and she graciously assisted in the preparation of this manuscript.

A number of books have been written for children about the Shoshone. Many of them are listed in the section of this book titled "To Find Out More." Detailed information can be found in the historical records on the official Web sites of various Shoshone tribal groups. Sharon Malinowski, Anna Sheets, and Linda Schmittroth edited the four-volume *UXL Encyclopedia of Native American Tribes*, which contains a very thorough account of the history, culture, and customs of the tribe. Also helpful were *American Indians* edited by Harvey Markowitz, *Encyclopedia of Native American Tribes* by Carl Waldman, and *Native America in the Twentieth Century* by Mary B. Davis.   —*Christin Ditchfield*

Index

Numbers in *italics* indicate illustrations.

About the Author

Christin Ditchfield is an author, conference speaker, and host of the internationally syndicated radio program, *Take It To Heart!* She has interviewed celebrity athletes such as gymnast Mary Lou Retton, NASCAR's Jeff Gordon, tennis pro Michael Chang, the NBA's David Robinson, and soccer great Michelle Akers. Her articles have been featured in magazines all over the world.

A former elementary school teacher, Christin has written more than forty books for children on a wide range of topics, including sports, science, civics, and history. She recently wrote young-adult biographies of Clara Barton and Louisa May Alcott for Franklin Watts. Ms. Ditchfield makes her home in Sarasota, Florida.